# HEATHER

by Thomas Eccleshare

## Cast (in alphabetical order)

Ashley Gerlach
Charlotte Melia

## Creative Team

| | |
|---|---|
| Director | Valentina Ceschi |
| Designer | Lily Arnold |
| Lighting Designer | Joe Price |
| Sound Designer | Iain Armstrong |

| | |
|---|---|
| Producer | Paul Jellis |
| Assistant Producer | Martha Rose Wilson |
| Stage Manager | Kerri Charles |
| Publicity Design | Luke W Robson |

An earlier version of *Heather (Helen)* was first commissioned by and presented as A Play, A Pie And A Pint production at Tobacco Factory Theatres and Òran Mór in 2014.

*Heather* is a co-production between Dancing Brick and Paul Jellis in association with Tobacco Factory Theatres and the Bush Theatre.

### Ashley Gerlach

Theatre includes: *Romeo & Juliet* (National Theatre); *Macbeth* (National Theatre); *You Forgot The Mince* (Imagine If); *The Events* (GEST); *All My Sons* (Talawa Theatre Company); *The Nutcracker* (Unicorn Theatre); *Dick Whittington* (Theatre Royal Stratford East); *Breaking Point* (Acting Out Productions); *Alice in the Walled Garden* (Sixteen Feet); *Borderline Vultures* (The Lowry); *The Legend of Captain Crow's Teeth* (Unicorn Theatre); *Where the Flowers Grow* (Warehouse Theatre); *7 New Plays by Young Writers* (National Theatre Studio); *Naked Soldiers* (Warehouse Theatre); *Herons* (Falling Leaves).
TV and film includes: *The Midnight Beast* (Warp Films for Channel 4); *Up!* (BBC); *The Manny Norte Show* (Hey Buddy Productions); *Rock and Chips* (BBC); *The Bill* (Talkback Thames); *A Dangerous Way to Live, Requiem* (Jaffa Films).

### Charlotte Melia

Theatre includes: *Genesis* (Soho Theatre/The Lowry); *The Window* (Bristol Old Vic); *I and the Village* (Theatre 503); *Never So Good, Afterlife* (National Theatre), *High Street Odyssey* (Inspector Sands/China Plate); *The Wasp* (Bristol Old Vic/New Wolsey); *Helen* (Tobacco Factory/Òran Mór); *The Common* (China Plate/Beaford Arts); *Wired* (Kings Head); *A Moon For The Misbegotten* (The Old Vic); *Cartography* (New Wolsey); *Much Ado About Nothing* (Ripley Castle/Sprite Productions); *The Miniaturists* (Arcola Theatre); *Hamlet* (ETT/New Ambassadors).
TV and Radio Includes: *Delayed Departures* (Radio 4); *The Lost Honour of Christopher Jeffries* (ITV); *Doctors* (BBC1); *The Art of Awkward Conversation* (Notebook Films).

### Thomas Eccleshare – Writer

Thomas Eccleshare is a writer, performer and theatre maker trained at the Jacques Lecoq School. He is the co-artistic director of award-winning visual theatre company Dancing Brick, with whom he has toured nationally and internationally. As a playwright he has won the Verity Bargate Award, the Catherine Johnson Award and been nominated for an Off West End Award for most promising playwright. He writes regularly for TV and film and last year was the recipient of the inaugural JJ BAFTA Screenwriting Bursary. He is currently on attachment at the Royal Court.

### Valentina Ceschi – Director

After graduating from Oxford University, Valentina trained for two years at the Jacques Lecoq School and the Laboratory of Movement Research in Paris, graduating in 2008. Since then she has been working in theatre, dance, live art and opera in the UK and Europe. Valentina is co-artistic director of Dancing Brick with Thomas Eccleshare with whom she has written and performed in all the company's shows, including the critically acclaimed *21:13*, the award-winning *6.0:How Heap* and *Pebble Took on the World and Won*, and *Captain Ko and the Planet of Rice*, touring nationally and internationally since 2008. Valentina works with new writers at the Soho Theatre and with experimental cabaret duo House Of Blakewell produced by Vicky Graham. She is associate director of Olivier Award-winning opera company OperaUpClose and co-founder of all-female design-led collective BraveNewWorlds. Valentina has worked with many different companies, theatres and opera houses including La Scala opera house in Milan. As a youth theatre director she frequently works with youth companies throughout the UK and is associate director with the National Youth Theatre. Valentina is currently on attachment at the National Theatre Studio with Dancing Brick developing a new show for young adults.

### Lily Arnold – Designer

Productions include: *Room* (Abbey Theatre, Theatre Royal Stratford East); *Snow In Midsummer*, *The Jew of Malta*, *King Lear*, *The Taming of The Shrew* and *The Rape of Lucrece* (RSC); *Broken Biscuits* (Paines Plough); *Forget Me Not* (Bush Theatre); *The Solid Life Of Sugar Water* (Graeae/National Theatre); *Beached* (Marlowe Studios/Soho Theatre); *The Edge of our Bodies*, *Gruesome Playground Injuries* (Gate Theatre); *The Sugar Coated Bullets of the Bourgeoisie*, *Peddling*, *So Here We Are* (HighTide); *Minotaur* (Polka Theatre); *Yellow Face*, *World Enough and Time* (Park Theatre); *The Boss of It All* (Assembly Roxy/Soho Theatre); *A Season in the Congo*, *The Scottsboro Boys* (Young Vic, Clare Space); *Happy New* (Trafalgar Studios); *Ahasverus* (Hampstead Downstairs) and *A Midsummer Night's Dream* (Cambridge Arts Theatre).
Forthcoming include: *Rules For Living* (ETT).
Find out more at lilyarnolddesign.com

### Joe Price – Lighting Designer

Joe trained at the Royal Welsh College of Music & Drama and received the 2015 Francis Reid Award for Lighting Design. He will light the JMK Award-winning production of *My Name is Rachel Corrie* at The Young Vic this autumn.

Credits include: *Fossils* (Bucket Club, UK Tour & Brits off Broadway NYC); *Let The Right One In* (Arts Ed); *Magnificence* (Fat Git, Finborough); *Heads Will Roll* (Told by an Idiot, Theatre Royal Plymouth); *How To Date A Feminist* (Laundry Productions, Arcola); *Some Girl(s)* (Buckland, Park Theatre); *Around The World in 80 Days* (Blue Apple, Theatre Royal Winchester); *Some People Talk About Violence* (Barrel Organ, UK Tour); *Dry Land* (Damsel Productions, Jermyn Street Theatre); *Alternative Routes* (National Dance Company Wales, Dance House WMC); *Animal/Endless Ocean* (Royal Court/National Theatre Wales/RWCMD, Gate Theatre); *Y Twr* (Invertigo, UK Tour).

## Iain Armstrong – Sound Designer

Iain Armstrong is a composer and sound designer based in Birmingham, UK. His work is presented internationally and spans sound design for theatre and dance, electronic music, multi-channel sound installation, and live electroacoustic performance.

Recent work includes music composition for Humanhood's *ZERO* (mac birmingham, 2016) and *Orbis* (Without Walls, 2017). Sound design for *The Whip Hand* by Douglas Maxwell (Traverse Theatre/Birmingham Rep, 2017); *Looking For John* by Tony Timberlake (Birmingham Rep, 2016); *Stories To Tell In The Middle Of The Night* by Francesca Millican- Slater (Birmingham Rep, 2016/17), REND Productions Howard Barker double bill *The Twelfth Battle of Isonzo* and *Judith: A Parting From The Body* (Arcola Theatre, London, 2015); *Heartbeats & Algorithms* by Jenny Lee (Soho Theatre, London, 2016); KILN's *A Journey Round My Skull* (2014), *A Journey Round My Theatre* (2015) and upcoming *Delightful* (Birmingham Rep, 2017).
iainarmstrong.net

## Paul Jellis – Producer

Paul Jellis is an award-winning independent theatre and events producer. His work encompasses new writing, multidisciplinary performance, interactive theatre and immersive experiences. He has worked with leading theatres across the UK including the Young Vic, Old Vic, Lyric Hammersmith, Sheffield Theatres and Birmingham Rep, and internationally in New York and Bangalore. His production of *Barbarians* at the Young Vic was nominated for an Olivier Award for Outstanding Achievement in an Affiliate Theatre. He has also developed and produced experiential events with global brands including Ray Ban, Courvoisier and PlayStation.

# TOBACCO FACTORY THEATRES

Tobacco Factory Theatres produces and presents excellent art in unique, intimate spaces, including in its Factory Theatre, as well as off site in Bristol and in venues across the country.

It presents a jam-packed programme of diverse and exciting shows, workshops and events, from classic and contemporary theatre, to theatre for families, comedy, dance, music, opera and puppetry.

It also programmes an extensive programme of engagement, learning and participation opportunities for audiences, artists and young people.

Tobacco Factory Theatres has forged an inspirational path to becoming one of the country's most respected venues in just 10 years. The diversity of the programme, combined with the astonishing average attendance capacity of 80%, make it one of the most well-attended, loved and popular theatres in the country.

Recent Tobacco Factory Theatres productions and co-productions include Caryl Churchill's *Blue Heart* (co-produced with Orange Tree Theatre, London), Conor McPherson's *The Weir* (co-produced with Sherman Theatre, Cardiff) and the Olivier-nominated *Cinderella: A Fairytale* (co-produced with Travelling Light, Bristol). Tobacco Factory Theatres was proud to co-commission an earlier version of Thomas Eccleshare's *Heather* (previously named *Helen*) as part of the A Play A Pie And A Pint series, co-produced with Glasgow's Òran Mór.

For more on Tobacco Factory Theatres and its productions, please see **www.tobaccofactorytheatres.com**

Tobacco Factory Theatres productions and co-productions are supported by the Tobacco Factory Theatres Production Fund. A small group of individuals have generously supported this fund to help Tobacco Factory Theatres to produce more of its own work. They are: **Founder Benefactors** Ken Edis / John and Susan Hart / Simon Inch / Ros and Cameron Kennedy / **Founder Patrons** Michael and Lynne Bothamley / **Platinum Patrons** Martin and Mary Bailey / Geoff Clements / Tim and Judith Lockwood Jones / Christopher and Sarah Sharp / Anna Southall / Helen and Peter Wilde / **Gold Patrons** Roger Corrall / John and Sue Cottrell / Alec Ewens / Unsal and Diana Hassan / Vivien Kies / Jo Luscombe McDonald / Chris Sims / P K Stembridge / **Silver Patrons** Judy Carver / Ruth and Stephen Illingworth / Alan Moore / Nisbet Charitable Trust

**Theatre Staff**
**Artistic Director** Mike Tweddle / **Executive Director** Lauren Scholey / **Director of Operations** David Dewhurst / **Head of Marketing** Becky Cresswell / **Marketing Manager** Hilary Coleman / **Marketing Officer** Ben Dunn / **Development Director** Stephen Last / **Development Officer (Individual and Corporate Giving)** Jen Warner / **Development Officer (Trusts)** Hannah Litherland / **Producer** Kerrie Burke-Avery / **Assistant Producer** Vic Hole / **Children and Young People Director** Ailie deBonnaire / **Technical Manager** Matthew Graham / **Technician** Jason King / **Operations Manager** Katy Wilkes / **Administrator** Rusti Fells / **Finance Manager** Elaine Grünbaum / **Trustees** Sarah Smith **(Chair)**, Andrew Allan-Jones, Bertel Martin, Kate McGrath, Mark Panay, John Retallack, Chris Sims, Anna Southall, Martin Wright

**Core funders**

**Registered Charity No.** 1097542

# Bush
# Theatre
## We make theatre
## for London. Now.

The Bush is a world-famous home for new plays
and an internationally renowned champion of
playwrights. We discover, nurture and produce
the best new writers from the widest range of
backgrounds from our home in a distinctive corner
of west London.

The Bush has won over 100 awards and developed
an enviable reputation for touring its acclaimed
productions nationally and internationally.

We are excited by exceptional new voices,
stories and perspectives – particularly those with
contemporary bite which reflect the vibrancy of
British culture now.

Located in the newly renovated old library on
Uxbridge Road in the heart of Shepherd's Bush,
the theatre houses two performance spaces, a
rehearsal room and the lively Library Bar.

 Supported by
**ARTS COUNCIL ENGLAND**
 h&f hammersmith & fulham

**bushtheatre.co.uk**

HEATHER

Thomas Eccleshare

# HEATHER

OBERON BOOKS
LONDON

WWW.OBERONBOOKS.COM

First published in 2017 by Oberon Books Ltd
521 Caledonian Road, London N7 9RH
Tel: +44 (0) 20 7607 3637 / Fax: +44 (0) 20 7607 3629
e-mail: info@oberonbooks.com
www.oberonbooks.com

A catalogue record for this book is available from the British Library.

PB ISBN: 9781786822505
E ISBN: 9781786822512

Cover design by Luke W Robson,
with photography by The Other Richard

Printed, bound and converted
by CPI Group (UK) Ltd, Croydon, CR0 4YY.

## THANKS

For Charlie and Rose – those games of Harry Potter squads
paid off.

Thanks to Ali Robertson and Emma Callandar for asking me to
write the play. To Jojo Townsend, Melanie Zaalof, Mike Tweddle
and everyone at the Tobacco Factory for getting it on in the
first place. To James Hogan, George Spender, James Illman,
Serena Grasso and everyone at Oberon for letting people read
it. To Charlotte Melia, Tim X Atack and Ashley Gerlach for
bringing it to life.
To Paul Jellis and Martha Rose Wilson for getting the play on and
out there. To Stewart Pringle, Madani Younis and everyone
at the Bush. To Lisa Owens, Jane Finigan and Lu Kemp for
reading and notes. To Lily Arnold, Iain Armstrong and Joe Price
for bringing everything to the table, literally. And, last but
not least, to Valentina Ceschi for raising the whole thing to
another level.

*Heather is a play written for two actors, A and B. The two actors don't play the parts as such, but rather deliver the parts to the audience. The fact of what the actors look like is sort of immaterial; indeed, in some ways the contrast between the voice in the play and the speaker in the room is the fun of it.*

*A and B don't necessarily have to be the same actor all the way through. You may decide it is most interesting if one actor always plays A. But you might think it's more interesting if she plays A then B then A again. Up to you.*

# 1. SELECTED EMAILS

**A**        Dear Ms. Eames,

Thank you for sending me the manuscript for *Greta and the Pen of the Necromancer*. I'm glad that Jonathan recommended me – he's a dear friend – so thank you (and him!) for those kind words.

To cut to the chase, I found Greta to be a revelation. If this is, as you say, your first novel, then I think you have a long career ahead of you! It's not perfect – there are some issues and characters I would like to discuss with you (I'm not certain about Drexler, the Lord of the Wolves, who feels a trifle derivative) – but overall I found it to be witty, sharply plotted and the characters charmingly drawn. I agree with what you said in your covering letter that it's not a 'children's book' but, in my opinion those distinctions matter less and less.

Would you be available to come to my offices in London to discuss the book? We would very much like to talk to you about developing and, hopefully, publishing it some time in the future?

All the best,

Harry Purville

**B**        Dear Harry,

Thank you so much for your kind words – I'm over the moon!

I probably shouldn't mention this but I have had a number of less enthusiastic responses from publishers so I can't tell you what it means to me to hear praise for Greta! I can honestly say she feels like a daughter to me so it hurts when people are mean to her ;)

Thank you also for mentioning your fears about Drexler. My original intention was to provide a threat to the Butterfly Fields and created Drexler to do this, but I agree that as it turned out, he felt a little tired. Instinctively I wonder if it might help if I took out his enchanted collar?

My only piece of bad news is that I won't be able to come to London to meet you. I am very pregnant (my other daughter ;) ) and don't feel comfortable being too far away from my doctor. Oh, and my husband!

If we could continue to talk via email for the time being that would be great for me.

All the best,

Heather

**A**      Dear Heather,

Thank you for replying so swiftly. Of course I understand about the pregnancy – I'm sure we can move forward without a visit if we're both happy.

In short, we would like to purchase the rights to publish the book. I would then handle the editing personally and we would work towards a final draft for publication. For all

2

this we would be able to offer you a £5000 advance set against the royalties.

If all this sounds palatable to you I will have our business affairs people get in touch with you and we can send a contract over ASAP.

All the best,

Harry

**B**     Hi Harry,

This all sounds wonderful – how exciting!

With any luck there'll be two great pieces of news within a few weeks of each other.

All the best,

Heather xx

**A**     Hi Heather,

Thanks for returning my call earlier, sorry you had to go but I appreciate time is short in the circumstances!

I hope all the notes made sense – please give me another call if you need to clarify anything.

Looking forward to the revised draft.

All the best and love to Caroline too,

Harry

**B**     Dear Harry,

Please find attached the new draft. Sorry for the delay, it proved a little more difficult than I thought – if only *I* had a magic pen!

All the best,

Heather

**A**     Dearest Heather,

I couldn't be happier, I think these changes have made the difference. I'm very happy to 'let the Dragon out of the witch's coven'!

H xx

**B**     Harry,

What happy news, I'm thrilled.

It couldn't come at a better time for me. I have been rather ill I'm afraid. Without going into details my doctor tells me it is quite serious. It certainly feels that way I'm afraid and I have been stuck in bed for the last few weeks. It's only Caroline and thoughts of the next Greta book that cheer me up.

Please keep me up to date with all the progress toward publication. I'm so excited and only sorry I can't be a part of it in person.

All the best,

H xx

**A**   Gosh Heather,

I'm so sorry to hear you're ill. Please don't let this be an extra stress on you. I have a lot of experience with this sort of thing so I'm sure we can handle things our end and of course we will keep you up to date with everything.

H xx

**A**   Dear Heather,

Attached is the draft of the cover – what do you think!

Personally, I'm in love with it. I think Serge has really captured Greta's spirit and the gold leaf is even more resplendent than I imagined it! What you don't get with the PDF of course is the fact that the motes of magic dust coming from Greta's pen will be slightly embossed.

I hope you're as pleased as we all are!

Lots of love,

H xx

**B**   Dear Harry,

It's everything I wanted.

Thank you,

H

**A**       Wonderful! Full steam ahead!

H xx

**B**       Dear Harry,

I've just received the books through the post!
What a wonderful surprise! I have been
feeling a bit down recently, not at all myself,
and this was exactly what I needed! I have
been staring at them ever since!

Well, that's eight gone, just need another
2992 to sell and we'll have to do a second
edition ;)

Love,

H xx

**A**       Dear Heather,

I hope you're feeling better, it was good to
chat, albeit briefly, just now, thank you for
calling.

Our initial offer to the major booksellers –
Waterstones, Tescos and Foyles so far – has
been met with a great deal of enthusiasm,
and Tescos in particular are interested in a
point of sale promotion, which would be
amazing for a first timer. As I mentioned just
now, Amazon are already getting a lot of
positive feedback on the message boards.

I don't want to get our hopes up but I have
to confess, the omens are good.

Fingers crossed,

Harry xxx

**A**     Oh Heather,

What a star you are! I hope you are making
progress with the second Greta book because
the first is, if you'll forgive the pun, flying!

The notices – we've had the *Times, Sunday
Telegraph* and the *London Evening Standard
Magazine* half term reads special so far – have
been glowing and, more importantly, the
word online is fantastic. Waterstones have
already ordered more and Amazon are
restocking too.

My darling – it's a hit!

I do hope you are well enough to come
down to London for a celebration meal –
Ian of course too if you can bear to leave
Caroline with someone – or if not I must
come up to you to raise a glass!

Harry

**B**     Dear Harry,

What fantastic news. I know I mustn't but
I'm already fantasising about private schools
and round the world trips for Caroline!

I'm afraid I really can't come to London
and I must insist that you don't come up
here. I hate to be so vain, but I just hate the
thought of my illness getting involved in all
this. I can't tell you how nice it is to have
something completely separate!

I hope you understand. Long may this continue,

Lots of love,

H xx

**A**     Dear Heather,

I hope you're feeling a bit better. I'm sorry to inundate you with calls when you're so fragile. It's hard to express quite how much demand there is for interviews or public appearances. Not to sound vulgar, but the fees alone – beyond the obvious help to publicise the book – are hysterical. I hope you're aware how much the Greta craze has taken hold. I have little girls (and not a few boys too) outside the office with their parents dressed in their homemade woollen forcefield hats trying to meet you. Sales, as I hope Jonti explained in his email with the revised contracts for the rest of the trilogy, are, frankly, unprecedented. I don't think I've ever seen anything like this happen so quickly.

I'm sure it has already occurred to you, but there will come a point when you will need to give an interview face to face. Emailed Q and As and quick phone interviews are great, but the honest truth is, either we do it ourselves, controlling the atmosphere, and with some influence over the tone, or some hack will track you down and knock on your door anyway. If you could have a think at least, that would be great. If not, of course I will do what I can to keep the 'mystique' alive!

Love to the family,

H xxx

Sent from my iPad

**B** Dear Harry,

I'm so excited that everyone seems to have taken Greta so firmly to their hearts. Thank you for forwarding all the letters, some are so cute! They really make me feel like I am sharing something with so many people and that they, if this doesn't sound too grand, understand and like a little part of my mind. It's a wonderful feeling.

I would really appreciate it if you could continue to refuse interview and appearance requests. With Caroline and how I'm feeling I would rather keep everything normal as much as I can. Even going online to read reviews is a bit much for me. Can the PR team keep up the 'reclusive writer' angle until I recover? Frankly it seems like sales have a good momentum all on their own, I wonder how much they need a helping hand from me!

I hope you understand,

H

**A** Hi Heather,

I hope you are feeling better. Everyone at the office is tremendously excited as the launch of book two approaches. Parker have just signed on to make commemorative pens! Not sure yet whether they'll be able to shoot out magic fire, though! ;)

I just wanted to say personally how excited I am that you'll be able to attend the launch event. We have come so far! People are so desperate to meet you! You deserve to feel the warmth of the embrace of your public!

Plus, I am looking forward to giving you a big hug and telling you with all my heart that working on your books has been the apotheosis of my professional life.

With love,

Harry.

PS. Attached are the revised contracts for the video game: Greta now won't be able to hold a gun, a knife, or any weapon other than the pen.

**B**      Dear Harry,

Thank you so much for your kind and heartfelt words. I'm so excited about the launch too and I hope it goes without saying how grateful I am to you and all the team for all the hard work you've done and are doing. You've believed in me and Greta since the beginning and I'll never forget that.

Unfortunately I have some bad news about the event. I dearly, dearly wish I could join you all for the launch but I'm afraid I must again disappoint you. I've taken a turn for the worse I'm afraid and found out this

morning that I have to begin some treatment
in a few weeks time that my doctor tells
me will be pretty heavy. I implored him to
let me travel down but he said he couldn't
promise it would not have a negative effect
on my health and of course I can't take any
risks. I have to think of Caroline.

I know this will be a disappointment to
everyone, but please be assured that it won't be
half as disappointing as it is to me. I'm gutted.

Yours,

Heather

**A**     Dear Heather,

I'm heartbroken. I've been trying to ring
you but can't get through. I have told the
team and, though I don't want to speak too
soon, we are making plans to try to move
the whole launch up to you. A street party
outside your house if need be. I don't want to
get your hopes up (it will cost a lot more and
it's a logistical nightmare) but the early signs
are looking good. Pam even thinks it could
be a great selling point and frankly there is
so much interest in you and the book that I
think the press would happily do the junket
in a nuclear waste facility if there were signed
copies and free egg sandwiches.

Give me a call to discuss.

Love,

H

**B**        Oh Harry please don't go to all this trouble,
I don't deserve it. I beg you not to move
the event. I'm ill and I look terrible and I
feel worse and I couldn't manage it. Really
I can't manage it. Harry I implore you as a
friend, please don't make me feel worse than
I already do.

Do the event in London. Let it be a success.
Let people read the books and I will get on
with writing the third.

H

**A**        My dear Heather, the last thing I want to do
is upset you. I have been trying to keep you
away from this as much as possible but after
your last email about the launch, the hype
surrounding the second book, the first film
about to come out, there is just too much
interest in you. It is too big a story.

I wish I could hold them off, I really do, but
I am increasingly worried that the price on
your head is too great.

The rumours on the internet, if you haven't
seen them yourself, range from insulting
to macabre. Only this week someone sent
me this link to a *Buzzfeed* article called *10
similarities between Heather Eames and Father
Christmas*. Number eight is 'only children
think they exist'.

I wish I could give you better news but this
is the truth my darling: they will find you.
And when they do we can't control them. If
we take control now, do a short appearance

at the launch, then *Piers Morgan's Life Stories* or something, that will be the end of it and you, Caroline and Ian can go back to living in peace.

Lots of love,

H


**B**      Dear Harry,

Thank you for being straight with me. I'm afraid you're right. I'm afraid they will find me eventually. I'm afraid once they do they might not like me.

That's just it you see... I'm afraid.

Could we not do more phone interviews? Or I could write another, longer autobiographical piece for a newspaper?

Thank you for trying to help, you're a dear friend,

Heather


**A**      Heather, what are you afraid of? What on earth is there not to like? Do you think the British public want some stuck up angel whose arsehole smells of talcum powder?

Don't be ridiculous! They want *you.* Exactly as you are. They want to tell you how much they love Greta! They want to share that love with you! They couldn't give a rat's arse if you have three heads and a moustache like Hitler on each one.

H

**B**          Harry you're hilarious.

I hope you're right. I suppose I am worried what they will make of me. I'm not what they expect you see. Although my arsehole does smell of talcum powder. Xx

**A**          What is it my dear? I promise you, it will be so so so much better than you think. Think what we have been through together Heather – you can trust me.

H xx

**A**          Please Heather, whatever it is, share it with me. I beg you.

H

**A**          Heather? Are you getting these? There's no answer on your phone and I haven't had a reply. Please darling, tell me what's on your mind.

**B**          Dear Harry,

I lied to you. I don't have a daughter.

I'm sorry,

Heather

**A**          Dear Heather,

Is that it! That's the secret you're afraid of! Honestly, Lord Byron was a sex-addict with a pet bear, I think people will forgive you a little fib.

What did I tell you – there's absolutely nothing to worry about! Shall I arrange a cosy interview where you can explain to people why you felt you needed to lie?

Xx

**B**     I don't have a husband. And I don't have cancer.

**A**     Ok. Like I said Heather, the British public have forgiven far far worse than a bit of lying. It might be a bit rough for a week or two but there's nothing people like better than a redemption story. I promise, everything is going to be ok. You have created something wonderful.

**B**     I'm in prison.

**A**     What?

**B**     My name isn't Heather Eames. This is just an email address I made. My name is Tariq Medjani.

I am sorry to have deceived you like this. I felt that a name like Heather Eames would be a better fit for the story. I don't know why. It was stupid.

**A**     Why are you in prison?

Why are you in prison?

If you don't tell me it will be impossible to control.

**B**      I killed three people.

**A**      No email in response.

**B**      I'm sorry Harry.

**A**      No email in response.

**B**      I was afraid. But I want to be honest now.

**A**      I need some time to think about this. I need to have a think about how to deal with this.

**B**      Two of them were children. I'm sorry Harry.

**A**      I need to think about this. Please just give me an afternoon to think about this. To work out a strategy. I need to talk to Pam and the PR team.

**B**      It was a mother and her children. They were a family.

**A**      Please Heather. I need to think. Please.

**B**      When it happened I was in a very dark place. I don't have an explanation but I was not well. Sometimes my mind would go to a place that was not me and I was unable to control it.

**A**      No email in response.

**B**   I followed her home after I saw her coming
out of Pizza Express on Hendon Way. I
pushed her through the door as she let
herself in. I was someone else.

I made love to her in the corridor.

Her children woke up and came downstairs.

They were panicking. I panicked.

I cut their throats open and then their
mother's.

That's the truth. I'm sorry Harry.

## 2. CONVERSATION

**B**     My house! My family!

**A**     I know.

**B**     My front door is covered in graffiti.

**A**     I know.

**B**     My house. My kids. My fami my fucking family I have two daughters and they are being bullied. Bullied.

**A**     What

**B**     They are six and eight.

**A**     do you want?

**B**     Six and fucking eight.

**A**     I'm sorry.

**B**     My Aston. My fucking Aston smashed up!

**A**     I know.

**B**     So when you sit there and you say why are you here this is why I'm fucking here this is why this. To tell you. To fucking to tell you.

A        Yes.

B        To see you.

A        Ok.

B        To

*Silence.*

A        It's ok.

B        I should smash your

*Silence.*

B        I should.

A        I know.

*Silence.*

B        And this coffee tastes like shit.

*Silence.*

B        And this is what you look like.

A        I'm sorry Harry.

B        Sort of what I imagined. Like sort of what I had in my head what I thought it would be.

**A**    Really I

**B**    Like what you wrote to me about when you saw the Greta film. It's what was in your head but at the same time something different.

**A**    The film.

**B**    And as soon as you see the real version the one you had in your head dies a little bit.

**A**    I couldn't watch to the end.

**B**    Just like I imagined. Tall.

**A**    Yes.

**B**    Strong.

**A**    Yes.

**B**    Male.

   *Beat.*

**B**    Dark hair. Less hair than I imagined.

**A**    Thanks for noticing.

**B**    More tattoos.

**A**    Hm.

**B**            More scars.

**A**            Yeh.

**B**            Fuck.

*Silence.*

**B**            Seriously fuck you.

*Silence.*

**B**            Fuck. Fucking. Fuck you. I should sm

*Silence.*

**B**            I didn't used to imagine you like that
                 obviously. I used to think you were, you
                 know, five two, mousy brown hair, reading
                 glasses, wonky teeth.

**A**            Yes. Well.

*Beat.*

**A**            For what it's worth

**B**            Mm?

**A**            You're going to laugh.

**B**            I doubt it.

**A**        I thought you were a man.

**B**        What?

**A**        All this time I thought, I don't know why, I
             assumed 'Harry'.

**B**

**A**        But here you are. Blonde bob. Pale skin.
             Expensive suit.

**B**        Thanks for noticing.

**A**        The guards probably think you're my wife.
             One of those pen pal–

**B**        What's that?

**A**        Nothing.

**B**        Jesus it's bad. You've been beaten up?

**A**        It's fine. It's normal.

**B**        They want money?

**A**        I guess. It's ok. I've got money.

  *Silence.*

**B**        Jesus this really does taste of shit.

A          You should try the food.

B          God help me.

*Silence.*

B          Tariq Medjani.

A          Yes.

B          Why didn't you tell me the truth?

A          Come on.

B          Why didn't

A          You know the first word I wrote

B          You just

A          Of the very first book?

*Pause.*

A          I read an interview with JK Rowling about how she came up with Harry Potter, you know. How she was on a train looking out the window and suddenly she saw all these wizards flying outside the window. How she was seeing these witches and wizards flying around and suddenly she realised that this boy Harry was sitting on the train. Like imagining it was actually him looking out of the window. Where was he going? What was he going to do? And suddenly she saw it all as clear as if they were all already written: the magic school, the arch enemy the whole fucking thing laid out.

**B**      So what was it? You were cutting some kid's throat and you thought, shit this would be a great chapter in a story about pre-pubescent witches?

**A**      Heather.

**B**      What?

**A**      Heather was the first word I wrote. I didn't have anything. No Greta, no Scorax, no Pen of the Necromancer, no story, no Code of the Ancient Witches. Nothing. I just wrote that word. H. E. A. T. H. E. R. And I thought, what comes next? What's lovely? What is the loveliest name in the world? Eames. Heather Eames. And then I was on the fucking train. I could see it all.

**B**      Scorax, Greta, the witches–

**A**      No. No that was all later. I could see Heather's house. I could see her husband. I could feel him inside me as they tried to have a baby – they'd been trying so long. I could feel her cancer growing, starting to corrupt her and kill her.

**B**      Jesus.

**A**   She had to finish the story quickly because I knew she was dying. She was dying as soon as she was born. She's the saddest character in the whole book.

**B**   And it just happened to sound, I don't know, female, white, English?

**A**   I gave the people what they want.

**B**   No.

**A**   Jaqueline Wilson, Gayle Forman, John Green. The biggest kids writers.

**B**   You underestimate people.

**A**   Jeff Kinney. Joanna Rowling. Are you beginning to notice something?

**B**   You killed a family. That's not prejudice, that's a fact.

**A**   And you think if it had been Heather, if it had been 'Heather Eames' who had killed that family

**B**   What are you

**A**   You think the people the papers you think the world would have had the same reaction being told that Heather Eames was a killer?

**B**          The name isn't important.

**A**          Or John Green or Jesse Andrews?

**B**          People reacted to the facts.

**A**          The facts are my name! My name changes
               the facts. And if you don't believe me then
               that's then you don't know

*Silence.*

**B**          Heather Eames. It's a lovely name.

*Silence.*

**A**          I want to show you something.

*Tariq puts onto the table a thick pile of printed pages. It's the
manuscript for the final Greta book.*

**B**          Tariq.

**A**          I know what you're going to say I've heard it
               but please just think about it.

**B**          I.

**A**          Look at it.

*Harry sighs.*

**A**          Hold it.

*Harry picks up the manuscript. It's the most beautiful woman she's ever seen. It's a work of art. It's a bar of gold.*

**B**          'Greta and the Cave of Shadows'.

**A**          Good title eh?

**B**          Harry Potter rip off.

**A**          Fuck you.

*She turns to the first page.*

**B**          Greta and the Cave of Shadows. By Heather Eames.

*Silence. She turns another page.*

**B**          Darkness had fallen right across the world, from the icy plains of the north to the southern deserts. It was midnight, and alone in her father's study at number 15B Acorn Street, sat a young girl, short for her age and with a dark brown ponytail that fell halfway down her back. She was staring at something in her hand. A small object, glittering in the light from her father's desk lamp. It was the pen he had given her before he died. The pen that only a few years ago she had

*She stops reading. She catches her breath.*

**B**          Jesus. I don't want to stop.

27

**A**        It's good Harry. I promise you it's good.

**B**        It's not about being good.

**A**        Put it out as someone else. Say you had it ghost written by primary school kids in deprived areas.

**B**        Tariq.

**A**        We'll give all the money to charity.

**B**        Look

**A**        We'll. We'll. Please.

*Silence.*

**B**        Our revenues are down nearly 20%.

**A**        I'm sorry.

**B**        It's not as much as we expected.

*Pause.*

**A**        People are still buying it.

*Pause.*

**B**        My office was picketed.

A          I'm sorry.

B          I've had death threats.

A          I know.

B          I've had to leave Twitter.

A          I can't

B          My daughters, my fucking daughters get
           bullied

A          I'm sorry Harry.

*Silence.*

B          They want to know what happens though.

A          Yeah?

B          Jesus the youngest can't sleep without her
           Greta doll.

*Silence.*

A          They were good weren't they?

B          Tariq.

A          They were though. They were fucking good.

29

**B**          Don't.

**A**          Its just, I haven't read the first two for a while
               so. Sometimes I do, you know, they let me
               have them sometimes. They're not always
               like I remember. It's funny. Like I wrote
               them they came out of this out of me but I
               still don't really know them like I can still be
               surprised.

**B**          They're not yours anymore.

**A**          Yeah.

**B**          They're their own thing.

**A**          It's the first time we see Scorax that always
               gets me. I always remember it differently and
               then when I read it I'm like ah. Yeah that
               makes sense, that's so much better.

**B**          I love that bit.

**A**          How did I do that the first time if I can't even
               think like that now?

**B**          It's a wonderful moment.

**A**          It's like it wasn't even my head, like it just
               came from someone else, dropped in.

**B**          Michaelangelo said that the sculpture was
               already in the marble, he just had to uncover
               it.

A               Bit pretentious.

B               I suppose.

*Silence.*

B               For me it's when Greta first finds the pen.
                The description of it 'glinting like a wolf's
                eyes in the window'.

*Silence.*

B               You're a monster.

*Pause.*

A               Yes.

B               You are an evil evil wicked man.

A               I know.

B               You have done unspeakable things, caused
                unspeakable turmoil.

A               I was ill. I am

B               Horrible.

A               Ill

B               Horrible. Just horrible things.

31

*Silence.*

**B**     And then.

**A**     I know.

**B**     And then this.

**A**     I am ill.

**B**     Where did it *come* from?

**A**     I know.

**B**     How did you do it? Do both. How did you
do both?

**A**     Release. I don't know. Release from
something. Escape.

**B**     God.

**A**     From something.

**B**     They are so beautiful Tariq.

**A**     Yes.

**B**     So so beautiful. When I read them to my
girls for the first time. When I heard their
breaths draw in as Greta found the pen.
When I felt their hearts flutter as she stepped
through the curtains and into Rossini's Clock

Shop. You gave that to me. You were there
with us, the two of us together reading telling
that story in my daughters' bedroom in my

**A**        I'm sorry

**B**        God in my daughters'

**A**        I know.

**B**        Sitting on the bottom bunk.

**A**        It is beautiful.

**B**        Inside my house.

*Silence.*

**B**        Horrible.

**A**        Why didn't you insist?

**B**        I beg your pardon?

**A**        Please, I'm a bit ill, I've just had a baby. You
knew that if you came to visit me you would
find something you didn't like. It was better
for you just to have the manuscript, and hope
that everything else went away.

**B**        I begged you to do a book tour. I sent
endless invitations to the launch, to do
interviews.

**A**        Whatever.

**B**        I phoned you. I thought I was speaking to
             you remember. Chatting shit to your sister in
             law. Some fucking housewife in Mill Hill.

**A**        You liked the story as much as I did. The
             middle aged woman

**B**        I hope you paid her I hope she got a slice.

**A**        Rejected by everyone else

**B**        Bullshit.

**A**        Until one genius editor a knight in shining
             armour

**B**        I was busy. I have a company to run. I can't
             just drop everything to go and have lunch
             with some pregnant first time writer just cos
             she can't be fucked to come down to see me.

**A**        Right.

**B**        It doesn't mean I thought she was a fucking
             serial killer.

**A**        I'm not a serial killer, they all happened on
             the same night, it was one incident.

**B**        For fuck's sake.

**A**     Shit like that matters ok at least describe it
accurately. You're supposed to be a fucking
editor.

*Silence.*

**A**     How many writers do you represent?

**B**     I don't know, fifty maybe.

**A**     And how many haven't you met?

*Pause.*

**B**     None.

*Silence. Harry looks again at the manuscript.*

**A**     It's the same story Harry.

**B**     Is it?

**A**     This doesn't change the story.

*Pause. Harry shakes her head. She can't.*

**A**     I've taken up embroidery.

**B**     What?

**A**     Yeah they run this class in here, it's called
Knitting Behind Bars. A woman comes in,

Lynn, and teaches us how to knit and sew and stuff.

**B**   They let you have knitting needles?

**A**   We make these she calls them Comfort Dolls. They're like I don't know like little teddy bears I guess little woollen dolls.

**B**   And then what?

**A**   I think she puts them on her blog. People buy them. The money goes to community groups and stuff.

**B**   Don't Tariq.

**A**   People do lots of people buy them. It's about rehabilitation. People like to think

**B**   Tariq

**A**   Think that there is recovery you know people want to have

**B**   I can't have this

**A**   Hope

**B**   Conversation

**A**   People believe in redemption.

**B**        Only people who don't know what you did!

*Pause.*

**B**        People buy a doll from a prisoner. Of course they do. That's because in their mind he's a misunderstood poor boy who got mixed up in a bad crowd and ended up shooting a drug dealer.

**A**        That's not

**B**        People buy these dolls because they can just make up their own criminal. You think someone will buy a children's book from a man who raped and killed a mother and her children?

**A**        I.

**B**        Tariq.

**A**        That wasn't me.

**B**        I'm sorry.

**A**        That wasn't.

*Silence.*

**B**        The Lego's been pulled.

**A**        That's a pity.

**B**          You'll still get paid.

**A**          What about the theme park?

*Pause.*

**A**          I am Heather. I still am.

**B**          Tariq.

**A**          Greta saved me.

**B**          I don't care. I can't care.

**A**          If you spoke to Lynn, you'd see, the Knitting
               Behind Bars it

**B**          It

**A**          Works, people care.

**B**          doesn't matter.

*Pause.*

**B**          It doesn't matter.

*Harry holds the manuscript.*

**B**          They were my daughters' age.

**A**          I can't I don't know

**B**          They could have been my little girls.

*Harry holds the manuscript.*

**B**          This will be the last time you see me.

**A**          Yes.

**B**          We'll still pay your royalties of course.

**A**          Thanks.

**B**          I'm sorry Tariq. I'm sorry things turned out
                this way.

**A**          Don't be. I am what I am. I've done what
                I've done.

**B**          Yes.

**A**          Good and bad.

**B**          Yes. Good and bad.

*Harry holds the manuscript. She can't stop looking at it. Silence.*

**A**          People will buy it Harry.

**B**          Yes.

**A**          It's the end of the story. People care what
                happens.

**B**          Yes.

*Pause.*

**B**          I've been talking to Warner Brothers. They
             want to go ahead with the third film. Do it in
             two parts you know.

**A**          People want to know how it ends.

**B**          Yes.

**A**          They want to know if Greta's safe. They want
             to know if she turns out ok.

**B**          Yes.

**A**          Harry?

*Harry looks at Tariq.*

**A**          That's why you came today isn't it?

**B**          Yes.

## 3. SCREENPLAY

A         EXT. THE MOUNTAINS OF THE
             NORTH

B         Helicopter shot of the mountains. They are
             cold, unforgiving and barren. The clouds
             rumble with the coming storm, obliterating
             the moon.

A         EXT. THE CAVE OF SHADOWS

B         In the centre of the mountain range,
             unmistakably jutting from the skyline is the
             largest mountain of them all.

A         As we wheel around it we notice that the
             deep crevices in the rock make up a pattern.
             It is unmistakable: hewn into the surface of
             the rock is the face of Scorax, her features
             contorted. Her mouth open.

B         This is the Cave of Shadows.

A         INT. THE CAVE OF SHADOWS

B         Darkness. The cave is illuminated only by
             the flashes of lightning from the raging storm
             outside.

             The walls are etched deeply with runes and
             old spells. Bad things have happened here.

A         CRASH.

**B**     A sound from the edge of the cave and
          GRETA pulls her top half onto the edge of
          the cave.

          Greta looks BATTERED and BRUISED.
          On her cheek is the still-bleeding wound
          from the Night Ravens. Her hair is tied up
          and her eyes are steeled.

**A**     GRETA: (under her breath) Come on, Greta.
          Come on.

**B**     With her last ounce of strength Greta hauls
          herself up onto the ledge, and collapses,
          breathing heavily.

          ECHOING CACKLES fill the room, then
          disappear.

**A**     Greta tenses, frightened, then grits her teeth.
          She's got to do this.

**B**     She pulls herself to her feet and as she does
          so we see some rubble from the cave floor
          FALL out of the mouth of the cave and into
          the night. Greta watches it fall and fall and
          fall until it disappears into the darkness.

**A**     Greta gulps.

**B**     In her hand she clutches the PEN OF THE
          NECROMANCER.

**A**     GRETA (CONT'D): T-O-R-C-H.

**B**    The pen SHOOTS out a shaft of brilliant LIGHT, illuminating the walls of the cave.

**A**    Greta GASPS.

**B**    Across every wall are etchings, carvings, runes and spells.

As she approaches with the torch the runes and carvings begin to MOVE like SNAKES across the wall. She sees snatches of words: REGRET, HURT, PAIN.

GRETA:

**A**    Sandy was right: the carvings move. That's why the graffiti on Ben's bedroom door had disappeared by the time we arrived.

**B**    Suddenly there is a SCREAM from somewhere inside the cave. Greta wheels round.

**A**    Ben?! Ben, I'm coming!

**B**    But before she can move there's a:

**A**    BOOM!

**B**    The wall bursts apart.

**A**    Greta stumbles backwards and then

**B**    S-H-I-E-L-D!

**A**     A shield grows from the pen as debris and
shards of rock fly past Greta's head.

BANG!

A large rock crashes against the shield and
knocks her to the floor, then… silence.

**B**     Rnnng.

**A**     She looks up and sees that her leg is trapped
underneath a pile of rocks.

Suddenly, there is the sound of
SCREEECHING. High and horrible, it
echoes through the cave and sends a shiver
down Greta's spine.

Greta strains to see a shadow moving along
the sides of the cave. It's coming towards her.

The shadow is high and thin and long.
And at the end of one of its arms, is a thin-
fingered, bony hand, holding… a pen!

**B**     No. No! NO!

**A**     A foot appears on top of the pile of rocks.
Then a leg. Then all of a sudden, standing
on top of the rocks at Greta's feet is the tall
towering, figure of…

SCORAX, her red eyes glowing in the
blackness.

**B**     GRETA: It's you.

| | |
|---|---|
| **A** | SCORAX: Yes. Are you surprised? |
| **B** | I don't understand, you're…? |
| **A** | Dead? |
| **B** | I saw you die. I saw you fall from the Cliffs of the Burning Moons. |
| **A** | That's true Greta. But did you see me land? |
| **B** | Wh-? |
| **A** | Did you see my body break? |
| **B** | No. |
| **A** | Did you see my head sink below the waves? |
| **B** | No. |
| **A** | Did you hear me cry for help or beg forgiveness? |
| **B** | You know I didn't. |
| **A** | Then how did you know I was dead? |
| **B** | I-? |
| **A** | You should know better than anyone Greta that death is not that simple. Ever since the |

first time we met, in the corridors of Rossini's Clock Shop, you've known. I live, Greta, because I live in you. I exist because I exist in you. Do you think it's a coincidence that I have a pen like yours Greta? Do you think it's a coincidence that we first met the day after your father died? The day you inherited the Pen of the Necromancer. Greta, I am your... SHADOW!

**B**     No! That's impossible! I'm nothing like you. I'm...

**A**     Good?

**B**     Greta stares at her. This can't be true. She's good. Isn't she?

**A**     We FLASH into her thoughts:

**B**     Greta's POV as she

– STEALS the potion from McKlusky's desk.

– BLASTS the Necromancer from the Thousand Mile Ridge

– LIES to Ben and Sandy about finding the emerald pin.

**A**     END FLASH. Greta gasps. It can't be. I've tried to be good.

**B**     Answer me this, then, you feeble, worthless worm: who was there the day you couldn't stop Ricardo falling from Harlow's Tower?

**A**    You.

**B**    Who was in your nightmare the morning before you betrayed Lord Scree?

**A**    You!

**B**    And whose shadow did you think you saw just before Ben disappeared?

**A**    But – how could you be in all those places at once? How could you change shape so quickly?

**B**    Well that's easy. The answer… is in your hand.

**A**    Greta looks to her hand. And in it, clutched in her fist, is her PEN.

My pen.

**B**    You never found out where it came from, did you Greta?

**A**    I…?

**B**    Your pen was carved from the tusk of the last Snow Stag. The Snow Stag was a beautiful creature. Its pelt was soft as January snow. It's eyes, dark and red as dying fire. The last of its kind was just a fawn. No bigger than a lamb it was and before it died it was hunted for days, right across the North. When it

was killed its blood stained the whiteness of
the snow in which it lay and its hunter took
his prize. The great tusk of the beast, more
magical and valuable than anything before
or since. And from that tusk he carved–

**A** A pen!

**B** No Greta. He carved... two! Your pen has
a dark twin. Hewn from the same father,
housed in the same bone, my pen and yours
are intertwined. You see Greta you think that
you are Good and I am Evil but I'm afraid
it's not that simple. I AM you. You ARE me.

**A** No! B-O-L-T!

**B** A lightning bolt shoots from the pen and
EXPLODES the pile of rocks. Greta rolls
free of the rocks that trapped her. Scorax has
been blasted to the other side of the cave.

**A** The two enemies scrabble to their feet and
face each other across the cave with their
pens out.

**B** What do you want?

**A** I want the second Pen of the Necromancer.

**B** Why?

**A** You have no idea of the force you wield
in your hand. All these years you've been

using it to conjure silly spells and children's magic tricks. To write little stories for your friends that make you feel *safe* and *happy* and stop you being scared of the dark – never knowing its true power.

**B**      What do you mean?

**A**      You really are so young Greta.

**B**      What can it do?

**A**      So young and so green.

**B**      Tell me!

**A**      The two pens bestow on their master the most precious power of all. The power to...

**B**      What?

**A**      Talk to the dead!

**B**      ZZZING! A bolt of lightning flies forth from Scorax's pen.

**A**      FFSHAA! A whoosh of air flies from Greta's.

**B**      The two witches are blown into the air by the power of the mutual blast. The two spells interlock and twist together.

**A**    The walls of the cave blow red, then blue, then
green with the magic of the combined power.

**B**    Greta and Scorax are raised up by the spell
and drawn together.

**A**    They are pulled closer and closer.

**B**    What's happening?!

**A**    Give me the pen Greta.

**B**    No.

**A**    Give me the pen!

**B**    The spell has overtaken them now,

**A**    They can't control it, but are within it,
without it, like atoms in a galactic burst.

**B**    Their bodies are drawn together. The walls
of the cave flex and stretch.

**A**    The words in the rock glow gold and black
and burst with fire. There is another BLAST
and Scorax and Greta are pinned next to
each other onto the floor of the cave.

**B**    They look up at the starburst of spells
coming from the two pens, now discarded
and floating in the air, humming and

vibrating from the power of the magic. They are both terrified.

**A** Still staring up at the starburst, their hands, almost without thinking, reach for each other

**B** and CLASP together.

**A** SCORAX: I can't control it.

**B** GRETA: I'm afraid.

**A** Me too. I'm afraid too.

**B** The light between the two pens glows

**A** and bends

**B** and begins to take shape. It is a small dot at first.

**A** Then the dot becomes a circle.

**B** Then the circle splits into two.

**A** And the circles become eggs.

**B** And the eggs stretch and grow until they are shapes they both recognise.

**A** GRETA: You were right.

**B** SCORAX: Yes.

A          GRETA: The dead.

B          The light is now two bodies. The bodies of
           two children, shimmering like liquid silver.

A          Children?

B          Yes.

A          Where is their mother?

B          I don't know.

A          Are they alive?

B          I-I don't know. This is deep magic. Old
           magic. I can't control it.

A          The pens – look!

B          The pens are floating above the outstretched
           palms of the two children. SCORAX: This
           is the prophecy of the Necromancer: the two
           pens will raise the dead to tell their story
           together.

A          FLASH! Fire flows from the pens and
           surrounds the children.

B          It jolts their bodies stiff. Slowly,
           incrementally, their mouths open.

**A**     And their mouths are as deep and as black as
          night.

**A** and **B**     There is a place. South even of the Cliffs of
          the Burning Moons. It is a place of infinite
          beauty, where the waves kiss the shore like
          a mother to her children. Where the sun
          nurses the forest so that it grows green and
          strong and vast. We love you. We love both
          of you. It's ok. It will be ok. We forgive you.